THE BITE-SIZED ENTREPRENEUR

"You can create the life you imagined and still be an entrepreneur. Damon's new book will give you the easy way to implement strategies and do just that. Entrepreneurship is the best gig ever only *if you do it the way Damon lays out. Otherwise, you'll be working for the worst boss you ever had."*

--Cameron Herold, author of Double Double *and* Meetings Suck

"For every would-be entrepreneur who's wondered if it's possible to "crush it" without crushing yourself, this book is for you! In this concise read, Inc. columnist Damon Brown lays out a road map for launching a satisfying and successful business without overturning the life you currently have."

–Meagan Francis, co-host, the LifeWork Podcast

i

"Sure, it starts with passion, but what do you know about living the life of an entrepreneur? The Bite-Sized Entrepreneur *gives smart, succinct advice about how to follow your business dreams, including why to treat Tuesday like Monday; the difference between busyness and productivity; and three effective ways of saying 'no.' Highly recommended for would-be entrepreneurs and freelancers."*

--Kelly James-Enger, *author of* Six-Figure Freelancing, Second Edition: The Writer's Guide to Make More Money

"A practical and actionable guide to accomplishing your goals that can help anyone master the mindset needed to become a self-made success."

–Scott Steinberg, *bestselling author of* Make Change Work for You

"In The Bite-Sized Entrepreneur, *Damon Brown lays waste to both the misconceptions and pesky little lies we tell ourselves about why we can't make our side hustles a reality. A thoughtful, provocative read, Brown will help you understand why you have more time than you think to follow your passions—and offers smart, actionable advice to help you implement the right strategies so you can make your side hustle successful within the boundaries of the life you live today."*

—Kayt Sukel, author of The Art of Risk *and* This Is Your Brain On Sex

Jenny,

Create today!

All my best,

D

ASDA'17

THE BITE-SIZED ENTREPRENEUR

21 WAYS TO IGNITE YOUR PASSION & PURSUE YOUR SIDE HUSTLE

Damon Brown
Inc.com columnist &
Co-Founder of Cuddlr
www.bitesized.biz

TWITTER/INSTAGRAM: *@BROWNDAMON*
CONSULTING & SPEAKING REQUESTS:
DAMON@DAMONBROWN.NET

PUBLISHED BY:
Damon Brown

The Bite-Sized Entrepreneur, 1st Edition
Copyright 2016 by Damon Brown
Edited by Jeanette Hurt
Cover designed by Bec Loss

*Some material has been graciously reprinted
or inspired by my work on Inc. Magazine
Online, within random tweets, and on
scribbled index cards. Thank you.*

To Alec,
who inspired me to do my first TED Talk &
build my first successful startup before he
could even speak.
Thank you.

"Most of us have two lives. The life we live, and the unlived life within us. Between the two stands Resistance"

-Steven Pressfield, The War of Art

READING

OTHER BITE-SIZED BOOKS

THE BITE-SIZED ENTREPRENEUR

(KINDLE, AUDIOBOOK ON AUDIBLE & ITUNES)

THE PRODUCTIVE BITE-SIZED ENTREPRENEUR

(PAPERBACK, KINDLE)

SELECTED BOOKS BY THE AUTHOR

OUR VIRTUAL SHADOW:

WHY WE ARE OBSESSED WITH DOCUMENTING OUR

LIVES ONLINE

PORN & PONG:

HOW GRAND THEFT AUTO, TOMB RAIDER

AND OTHER SEXY GAMES CHANGED OUR CULTURE

PLAYBOY'S GREATEST COVERS

THE DAMON BROWN READER

A Word on Passion

Passion is the compass that points you in the right direction above the fog of the moment and the uncertainty of the future. Passion is also the instinct that pushes you to destroy everything else to get that brass ring.

Passion will leave you stranded if you do not put in the time. Passion will also give you the heart of steel needed to thrive when the less dedicated will falter.

Passion is our vice and our victory. Use it wisely.

Introducing You, the Bite-Sized Entrepreneur

I never intended to be an entrepreneur. I just had an idea.

At the time, I was a freelance tech journalist living in San Francisco. A friend of mine was struggling to remember a quote. I asked, innocently, "Isn't there an app for that?" There wasn't, and I found myself turning into an entrepreneur for the same reason most creators do: I realized something I needed did not exist and, if I didn't create it, it might never exist.

The odd part wasn't the journey to creating what would become the app So Quotable: it was who was actually making the journey. I wasn't a young, hooded Harvard dropout like Facebook's Zuckerberg, nor was I a brash, brilliant college dropout like Apple's Jobs, nor a rich, hip L. A. kid like Snapchat's Spiegel.

I was a journalist and author, an African American man in his mid-30s who, aside from negotiating rates with magazines, had no business experience.

In fact, at the time, I was about to propose to my now-wife. By the time So Quotable ramped up to launch three years later, I had bought my first home, married that long-time girlfriend, and we had our first kid. In the midst of the launch, a colleague helping out on the tech side bailed, and I found myself learning Apple's iPhone programming language with one hand while rocking my newborn in my other, spare arm.

I wasn't sure if the app – or even I – would make it to the finish line, but I also had not felt so alive in a long time. I'd wake up in the middle of the night with new ideas and realize elegant solutions to my app challenges during dinnertime. It was like I had two babies instead of just one. It was the passion to make my mark: I wasn't staying up late and getting up ridiculously early to watch my favorite show or to have "me" time. It was a nobler cause.

I was also doing things my way. Instead of staying in Silicon Valley, ditching my girlfriend, and dressing like a college student, I moved out of Silicon Valley, settled down behind my proverbial white picket fence, and created the type of entrepreneurial life that *I* envisioned.

And, to my surprise, it worked. So Quotable launched in time for my first TED talk and gained a great cult following. The success connected me with two others to launched Cuddlr, a social plutonic app for connecting for hugs. Cuddlr hit #1 on the Apple App store twice, got us on the cover of *The Wall Street Journal*, and was acquired less than a year after it arrived. I handled the Cuddlr launch through daily 4 a.m. Skype calls with my international colleagues, with occasional breaks to coax my new toddler back to sleep.

The truth is that the success didn't happen with the media coverage, the TED talk, or even the Cuddlr acquisition, but from doing and completing the work. As they say in Silicon Valley, real creators ship – and the product shipped! As soon as I met someone, told them about So Quotable, and said "You can download it off the Apple App Store now", I won.

You absolutely have the ability to follow your passion, fulfill a public or personal need, and make a legacy for yourself within the structure of your 9-to-5, your family life, or your daily grind. Never before have we been more capable to pursue our passions within the time we have. Like kids jumping double dutch rope, we have more room for our dreams than we think – it's just a matter of good strategy and timing. And perhaps that side hustle we create will become the foundation for the rest of our careers.

Bite-sized entrepreneurs incorporate brilliant startup techniques into their daily lives, giving themselves the focus and drive to pursue new passions while still being true to where they are in their personal and professional needs. *The belief that you have to sacrifice your livelihood to leave your entrepreneurial mark is a lie.* It isn't about losing the life you have, but adding value to create the life you want.

There are many things a bite-sized entrepreneur is not. She is not a dilettante, dabbling in various pursuits to combat boredom or gain prestige; a bite-sized entrepreneur doesn't give up when things get difficult. She is not a shallow businessperson, keeping the dedication superficial; a bite-sized entrepreneur dedicates every available ounce of free time to understanding her passion. She is not an obligated creator, getting her ego too invested into the idea to change; a bite-sized entrepreneur gives her passion space to transform organically into the business it was meant to be. Finally, she is not a patient person, assuming that one day she'll have all the time in the world to pursue her true passion; a bite-sized entrepreneur ain't waiting until retirement.

I'd love to be your guide on your entrepreneurial journey. Like my *Inc. Magazine* online column that inspired this book, I am giving you simple, digestible, and actionable insights that can be interwoven into your current life structure. You can flip through the 21 strategies in any order, though you may notice a natural flow if you read it straight from top to bottom. All of these ideas are explored with people who have successfully executed what you currently feel: A calling to create something bigger than yourself within the parameters of your current life.

Everyone's journey is different, which is the point: Realizing your business aspirations is not, and should not, be a one-size-fits-all process.

Let's make an impact on our own terms. Today.

-Damon Brown, August 2016

"Rule of thumb: The more important a call or action to our soul's evolution, the more Resistance we will feel towards pursuing it."

-Steven Pressfield, The War of Art

1
THE PASSION TRAP
Passion favors sweaty palms

Are you waiting for inspiration? Passion? A muse? I wouldn't count on it. When it comes to business, particularly entrepreneurship, you're better off leaning on just doing the work.

Artist and entrepreneur Jessica Abel describes the process well:

Passion for a practice or a subject comes from your investment of time and energy. Whatever your passion turns out to be is a combination of what you're into, your circumstances, and what happens to fall across your path, added to what you decide to spend your time on and what you're willing to take risks to do more of, with a just a tiny dash of natural talent.

The term "practice" has a double meaning. We have you practicing something every day, like playing the piano. We also have you doing the practice, as in growing the mental and emotional discipline to stay committed to a goal. It's not a coincidence that the same word is used in daily rituals and commitments, like meditation.

The truth is that passion will not get you out of bed every morning. Like love, it can be fickle and moody and fairweather. Passion makes you more susceptible to burnout and extreme thinking.

Doing the work, though? It sustains you, because it never changes, and it gives levity when things are great and when things suck.

All you have to do is show up every day.

2
LIES WE TELL
Be gentle with others, give yourself tough love

We all share common challenges when it comes to the tough road of entrepreneurship, but we also give common comforts to ourselves to push into another day.

In short, we lie to ourselves.

You don't know if the rockstar client will come through, a successful fundraise will happen or even if a larger competitor will snuff you out. There has to be a suspension of disbelief--otherwise, you wouldn't attempt to run your own business in the first place. Passion sometimes needs a little help trumping common sense.

There's absolutely nothing wrong with having faith in the future, but it is crucial that we recognize the times when we're placating ourselves for self-management. Here are the biggest comforts I say to myself. Perhaps you can relate.

I'll start this project/this business when I have more bandwidth

There is always tomorrow--until there is not. Like becoming a parent, there will never be an ideal time to launch your business. You will always need more resources than you have, more time than you got, and more energy than you can muster. If Steve Jobs, Elon Musk, and other visionaries waited until everything was perfect, then we wouldn't be talking about Jobs, Musk and their contemporaries right now.

As wine seller turned successful entrepreneur Gary Vaynerchuk said in an impassioned message: "I worked weekends and holidays every day starting at fourteen years old to make [my business] happen. I think back to all the time I put in of real, hard work before I saw any of the benefits." Don't wait for a red carpet.

I'll save my business/my finances if I can just net this one client
One client often isn't enough to save your business. Worse, if you put all your focus on netting one client, all things tend to fall to the wayside (even if you do get the client).

For instance, if your company gets any acquisition or investment interest, it is easy to start focusing on the potential payoff rather than the day-to-day work and the long-term strategy. And if it falls through, your company will take a while to get back on course--assuming it ever will.

I'll stay up all night/skip today's meals because that's how you crush it
Entrepreneurs will have you believe that skipping that night of sleep or "crushing it" all day without eating is the key to success--there is even a

startup or two dedicated to the idea. Sacrifices need to be made (I definitely walk the walk on that one), but there is no real correlation between depriving your body of needs and creating the next unicorn startup. In fact, you are more likely to burn out. Pushing yourself beyond your limits should be viewed as a contextually necessary evil, not as a default.

Consider this: If you do successfully reach that fundraising/monetization/users goal, then you'll have another goal after that and a business that will demand even more from you. I know many an entrepreneur who flamed out before reaching even the first milestone, defeating the whole purpose of moving forward. We often work harder than we should because we want to feel like we're crushing it--and that feel is more important than the actual impact. There is a difference between killing it and killing yourself.

I'll get work done on the plane/vacation/break

There is always more work to do: Another email to send, another pitch to perfect, and another glitch to correct. A major challenge is allowing ourselves to get away. The second part of the challenge? Letting others allow us to get away.

We assume we'll get work done on the flight in or during our travels, so we start pushing work into that so-called free time and start making promises that we may not be able to keep. It usually has one of two outcomes: You actually begin to relax after you realize how exhausted you are, but carry the guilt of making promises you won't keep, or you stress yourself out juggling the demands of travel and the needs of work, not really resting and, likely, not doing your best work because you are tired. Sometimes when you try to do two things, you actually fail at both.

I'll work with this PITA client one last time

Stop lying to yourself. Money, sympathy, or even status quo can compel us to repeat a client who is a pain in the ass (PITA). When we get another opportunity to work with the client, we tend to forget about the issues that stressed us out in the first place-- like parents deciding to have another kid. It's not until you're knee-deep in the same situation that you say, "Ah, that's why I swore I'd never work with them again."

Assume that you'll get another, better client (or clients) to replace them. Our fear is often driven by the feast or famine cycle: Keep every client you have, as you don't know when you'll get another one! In reality, we can't actually get new, quality clients if we're spending all our time inefficiently catering to our ill-fitting ones.

I need to quit my job/end my relationships so I can truly dedicate myself to my big idea

Kids will come, money will go, and jobs are necessary, but time is the one asset you can't get back. Waiting for a big chunk of time is usually a waste of time. You fall into the extreme thinking trap: You need to go big or not go at all. There are certain times when you have to leap, but that's usually after you've already recognized an opportunity and have done the homework... and that work takes time.

Keep in mind that Twitter, Yammer, and other billion dollar companies began as side projects founders did while focusing on their day job. Imagine if they waited until they could "go big". Plant the seed today.

3
EFFECTIVE PROCRASTINATION
What you aren't procrastinating on is more important

Procrastination is a bad, four-letter word, something to be avoided at all costs. For entrepreneurs, it is a sin somewhere between working for free and being a poor networker. I recently heard a quote, though, that changed my outlook on procrastination:

"The work you do while you procrastinate is the work you should do for the rest of your life." - Jessica Hische

Procrastination is usually viewed as the absence of work (and, therefore, the loss of profit and productivity), but what if it was a compass to your true calling? Perhaps the things you do that make time fly by faster can be integrated into your actual work.

In retrospect, the procrastination idea

has already changed my career. I was perfectly happy researching and writing books, but writing my first major book, *Porn & Pong: How Grand Theft Auto, Tomb Raider and Other Sexy Games Changed Our Culture*, on the history of sexuality and video games, put me on my first book tour. It was amazing! I spent five years working in solitude, and now I was finally able to discuss my theories and share my inside stories with the world. In fact, I began to enjoy the in-person intimacy more than the actual writing. I could have ignored that impulse and gone back to writing, but instead I shifted my focus to public speaking and soon got onto the TED stage doing more of what I love.

I would delay getting back to my writing so I could connect with people. Now I craft dynamic speeches in addition to writing books, turning my procrastination vice into my strength - and integrating my previous career into it in the process.

Here's how you can turn your procrastination into a powerful tool:

Listen

What activity are you doing now to prevent you from going back to the work you claim to enjoy? Mindless activities, or what you do without feeling stressed, could represent you going on instinct rather than forced action. In other words, figure out what you do in your life that feels natural.

Distill

What are the basic traits of your procrastination? Write down what you actually get from the activity. My love of long conversations boils down to connecting with others, getting different viewpoints, and arguing new ideas. Think about your own favorite procrastination and distill it down to two or three things you get out of it - without judgment.

Pivot

How can you integrate your natural

inclinations into your practice? For instance, if you love sitting in a coffee shop talking for hours, then perhaps you need more face time with your clients. It doesn't mean you have to change your entire business, but that you are pivoting to include more of what you actually love.

How can you integrate your favorite procrastination into your business life?

4

IDEA DEBT

Too many ideas mean none get done

I recently did an idea purge. I love committing my thoughts down onto index cards since they are simple, portable, and easy to organize. I started decluttering over recent months and I realized my pile of cards has gotten out of hand. The most amazing discovery: A new idea I thought I came up with was written on a piece of paper from a year before! Talk about going in circles.

If I could have smacked myself in my own head, I would have.

Author Kazu Kibuishi has a great term for this psychological weight: **Idea debt**.

I try not to look at what I'm going to do as this amazing great grand thing. I'm not just fulfilling some old promise that I made a long time ago. Now I'm actually solving problems in the moment, and that's so much more exciting than trying to fill years of what I like to call my "idea debt." That's when you have this dream of this awesome thing for years. You think, "Oh, I'm going to do this epic adventure. It's going to be so great." The truth is, no matter what you do, it will never be as great as it is in your mind, and so you're really setting yourself up for failure.

Kibuishi is talking about perfectionism: Waiting for the perfect time to start the perfect idea. Entrepreneurs (and, in a tip to my background, journalists) can't have this perfectionist approach because we A) have to bow to bigger deadlines, and B) we would never survive as entrepreneurs. Point me to a founder who believes her product is perfect to ship and I'll show you someone who won't be a founder for long. There are always more ways to improve a product or service. Getting to market is the only reason why we should stop.

If perfectionism isn't the big problem for entrepreneurs, then what is the issue? Idealism. Underlying Kibuishi's description is the idealization, the grand structure, the bells and whistles of our great scheme. And the idealization, structure and bells and whistles of another great scheme. Oh, and the other one we have, too. As entrepreneurs, we often have too many things planned out that weigh on our daily lives. At least for me, the "cool ideas" I have are far outweighing the time, energy and, frankly, quality control I'm able to muster.

So, ideas are getting killed. Slaughtered. Put out to pasture. Index cards have been chucked, unfinished manuscripts have been tossed, and untouched research has been recycled.

I ask three questions with every jotted note:

Why haven't I executed on it yet?
Again, I found ideas from a decade ago. From my passionate productivity to my sacrifice of sleep, I've managed to pursue and complete many goals. Chances are, there is a legitimate reason why this idea is on an old scrap of paper versus being a properly executed plan.

Why am I holding on to it?
Often, the idea of something is way more powerful than the will to create it. And if it is that powerful of an idea, then it will come back stronger after you dump it.

Why am I defending it?
By keeping that idea lingering you have to, by nature, defend it against criticism from others and even from yourself - otherwise, the idea would have been forgotten long ago. Unfortunately, we are so encouraged to defend our ideas and our beliefs, it's easy to neglect that we've outgrown them. And those ideas take space from potential new projects.

As I've purged my unfinished, incomplete ideas, I've realized how much ego I have tied up into what *could* be.

What idea should you be letting go?

5

BUSYNESS
Be productive, not busy

Projects, people, and passions can keep us on the move, but there is a distinct difference between busyness and productivity. Productivity feels like you do not want to stop. Busyness feels like you cannot stop.

Chronic busyness is rampant today, even though we know that it isn't good for us. Why do we keep ourselves excessively busy? There are three big rewards we get out of it:

Fulfills the ego
Like sociologist Brene Brown's take on comparative suffering, our busyness has become an acute measurement of our entrepreneurial worth: "You stayed up all night? I've been up for 72 hours straight working on my business." What we tend not to brag about is efficiency, as the wiser person may have paused,

strategized, and executed the same goal in a shorter period of time. It is definitely the age of the hustle, but I'd love to see us upgrade to the thoughtful hustle: How can we maximize our time? Busyness for the sake of busyness isn't it.

Fulfills the guilt

Feeling guilty when we actually do take a break is common, particularly during crucial periods. Even notable entrepreneur Elon Musk famously said he is afraid of vacations. However, it is during the pivotal points in your business where you actually need to pace yourself to stave burnout. You can minimize your guilt by having a structure in place that actually allows your business to continue uninterrupted while you are away.

Fulfills the silence

Being still often scares us, as it can make us feel anxiously bored and even to think about the things we've been avoiding with busyness. There is so much to be discovered when we allow ourselves to stop and quiet down. In fact, we may suddenly be given an elegant answer to the challenge we've been so busy trying to conquer.

6
A GOOD BURNOUT
Always maximize your time on the sidelines

If there is one thing we don't talk about in entrepreneurship, it is burnout. Company failure, spousal abuse and self-destroying habits are often accepted, but you're not allowed to admit you are exhausted. I know people who were so burnt out that they just disappeared without a trace. No judgment from me: I walked the precarious line myself, juggling raising my baby, bootstrapping a top Apple app, and maintaining my writing career.

No one is Superman or Wonder Woman. It's a shame that we don't talk about burnout more because, like the proverbial dark night of the soul, there are some amazing, priceless gems we can gain only in the space between ending and doing. Keep these strategies in mind, particularly if you can actually make time to process your burnout.

Stop
Burnout means you don't have the energy or focus to continue on. It means excessive late nights, drawn-out meetings, and extra drama have to go away, simply because you physically, mentally, and emotionally can't carry the weight. Good! They shouldn't have been there in the first place.

In my reflective time after my startup was acquired, I've done judicious editing in my life: removing excess, ending relationships, and pausing action. Decisions are now based on gut, even if that means missing opportunities. Urgency is as addictive as envy, and just as deadly, since it is the comparison to the person you think you deserve to be as opposed to the comparison to the competitor you think you see. A forced pause makes you reconsider where you put your energy, since your stamina is now limited.

Restrategize

What are you actually working toward? The day-to-day grind leaves little to no room for actual strategy, as you've got real, tangible business problems at your doorstep. The problem is that you don't restrategize until you or a loved one gets sick, your career takes a left turn or... you suffer burnout. Burning out shouldn't be looked at as a failure, but as an internal switch going off to tell you the parts of your life that have been neglected need to be attended to. It might feel like the timing couldn't be worse, but it is always the right time for your body, mind, and soul.

The only way forward is to make career decisions more conducive to the life you need. As Warren Buffett famously said, the most valuable thing entrepreneurs can say is "No." What stuff are you carrying that you shouldn't have been carrying in the first place?

Prioritize

Like when I was guiding the growth of my startup, my time is limited to what must be done *now*. However, unlike an overflowing email box or an app update demanding my attention, the things that are demanding my time are my sons, my intuitive leaps toward new ideas, and my own personal balance. I'm still running on a compressed time schedule, except it isn't filled with work, but with self-care. In a sense, I'm still taking in the last startup roller coaster ride -- at least emotionally. And I'm already gaining more clarity on my higher purpose as an entrepreneur.

Whether your hamster wheel is a startup or a corporate gig, we all struggle to prioritize. Instead, we triage based on the values we had before we got on the ride -- prioritizing based on an outdated model that doesn't take into account anything we've learned before. Been doing the same thing for five years without a break? Then you are organizing and prioritizing your work, and your career, based on whatever you learned a half decade ago. It is difficult to take everything in while you're trying to put out the next fire, but it's not impossible.

Burnt out? Embrace it as much as you can. The next journey will begin soon enough.

7

CLUTTER

New opportunities can't come in without space

My office is filled with lots of mindfulness and strategic tools, but the most useful one is a brand-new shredder. It cost $50 with coupons. Powerful enough to eat through papers, folders, and credit cards for 30 minutes straight, the little monster turned my save-for-a-rainy-day piles into buckets of confetti. The debris filled two garbage cans roughly my height and width.

What are you still carrying that you don't need? The cathartic act of destruction, of removal, and of closure gives us space for our next act. It forces us to make peace with the past. It also gives us pause to honor what we've done.

The physical clutter
In one pile, for instance, I found my

business card from a few years ago. It said JOURNALIST in big letters, proudly referred to publications that don't exist anymore, and highlighted projects and books that, at the time, represented the peak of my career. Speaking at TED was still a dream. Being a startup founder wasn't even on the radar. This random scrap piece of paper represented an acknowledgement of my growth, something that we entrepreneurs are want to do. It also made me realize that I was just as likely to find my 2016 business card one day and quietly acknowledge, again, how much my career had evolved–an inspiring, high-level thought while I do the day-to-day entrepreneurial march.

The virtual clutter

It can be just as inspiring to do a virtual purge. In fact, the real challenge in the future won't be us drowning in papers, but being overwhelmed by stuffed email accounts, bursting app screens, and bloated cloud drives. As I argued in *Our*

Virtual Shadow: Why We Are Obsessed with Documenting Our Lives Online, "The way we are using technology, our idea is that we document everything now and sort it out later." Well, the sooner you make "later" happen, the more mental and emotional space you'll give for future growth.

It's overwhelming, but here is where you can start:

- **Buy a shredder or another efficiency-focused product.** It's worth getting services and products that will create room for your future business. The virtual side is equally important. For example, a computer efficiency program can delete orphaned data and compress your useful files so you can work faster.
- **Take an afternoon to assess.** Imagine you are working in a new office on a new computer. We have unparalleled focus, clarity, and

relief when we're working with a clean slate. Decluttering and deleting isn't on the same level, but spending three hours organizing can bring us much closer to that nirvana. Time is our most valuable asset, but the return on investment here is high.

- **Prevent indecisiveness by hiding your stuff.** If you are on the fence about tossing any physical or digital goods, try putting them away, like in a dark part of the closet or in a file deep within your computer memory. Check in a few months later. If you haven't accessed them, then you probably don't need them. The hiding technique is popular among clothing decluttering experts.

Sorting, removing, and tossing our entrepreneurial baggage may the ultimate way to assess our past–giving us clarity for which previous pitfalls to avoid and where we should be focusing on next.

When is the last time you cleared the decks?

"During the process of rising, we sometimes find ourselves homesick for a place that no longer exists. We want to go back to that moment, before we walked into the arena, but there's nowhere to go back to."

-Brene Brown, Rising Strong

8
GROWTH SPURT
Take extra care during any transitions

I am in a growth spurt, just like my toddler. My favorite entrepreneurial clothes, which fit perfectly yesterday, are ridiculously small today. Ideas are moving faster than my attention span can handle. I need more rest, yet I'm overstimulated by all the possibilities now. I've outgrown my past and am stretching hard to build my future. "Comfortable" is a word I haven't used in a very, very long time.

You could argue that entrepreneurs are always in a growth spurt, but that's not really true. You cannot always be expanding, changing and breaking your foundation, and as much as our ego wants us to believe we're always pushing boundaries, it isn't possible to be in a continual state of growth. In fact, not pausing to evaluate can actually hurt our progress. No, a growth spurt is when you are expanding your customer base to a new demographic, you are pivoting your company to a new arena or you are moving your business to another level. It is scary, frustrating and exhilarating.

I see it every day when I am with my toddler, just as I see it every day when I look at myself in the mirror. Here's how I take care of both of us:

Feed yourself well
You don't know what you're doing anymore, so everything takes more time and energy than planned. Let's face it: There is a certain amount of autopilot that happens when we have a good rhythm going. Now, that rhythm is gone.

Like a growing child, your appetite is absolutely insatiable. In the past six months since selling my startup, I have read more books, been more thoughtful and asked more questions than any other time in recent memory. Why? I'm spending every moment figuring out how the hell to structure this next phase. My brain needs to be fed.

Give space

Similar to my son, you need an unusual amount of space to grow. Unlike him, however, you already have responsibilities, obligations and patterns that can keep you from growing into better opportunities. For you, me and other adults, we gain space by saying No. A lot. (Actually, that's not too different from a toddler, either.)

It wasn't until well after I transformed from journalist to entrepreneur that I realized how much I needed to remove from my life: From restructuring my relationships to chucking out outdated ideas. To flip Shonda Rhimes' TED Talk celebrating her year of saying yes, creating a Year of No is one of the best things you can do for your business.

Follow desire

What risks did you want to take now that you were too afraid or unable to take before? The beautiful part about instability is that one smart, calculated risk could be as disruptive as two or three calculated risk - no matter how many changes you make, you know you will never be the previous person again. The past is gone and cannot be rewound. The previous rules don't apply anymore.

Passion is your only clear compass.

9

FAVORS THE PREPARED
Make a contingency plan for success

How do you prepare for failure? It makes sense to have a Plan B, like a nest egg you can crack if it all goes south, or a set vocation that you know is in demand, or perhaps an alternative business you can launch. Only the most risk-tolerent - and, perhaps, reckless - of us go into an endeavor without any type of security. In fact, it may be more motivation for you.

Now, how do you prepare for success? I've found that most of us have made peace with failing, but actually don't have a plan for when we succeed.

In 2014, I co-founded the social meetup app Cuddlr with a couple other people - super small operation with barely a budget. I spearheaded the launch strategy and mapped out our plan from pre-launch to about six months out. My co-founders expected a cult following, I expected a more mainstream opportunity. What we got was a smash hit, getting an incredible amount of press and running to the top of the Apple App store within its first week. We're lucky we had a framework plan for post-launch, but it was difficult to ride the rocket ship even with that. Imagine if we had no plan for success! We probably wouldn't have been acquired.

The challenge for my co-founders and me, as well as many entrepreneurs, was that our focus was on evangelizing our service. But what if people love our service? It becomes preaching to the choir. There has to be a strategy if you actually win. It's akin to a presidential candidate being focused on the debates, but not having a set plan for when she actually gets into office. It's a recipe for disaster - even though you got what you wanted.

Here is some food for thought.

Plan it all the way through

What if you get that gold-star client or make that financial goal this year? Consider the next goal you have in mind. For instance, what kind of maintenance will be required to keep that hard-to-get client? Or how, exactly, will you be using that additional profit from a financial milestone?

Line up your mentors

A fresh success often means dealing with new issues that require a brand new strategy. Do you have a brain trust ready? The key isn't to have people who know what you know, but know what you'll need to know once you succeed. Again, planning for success means you assume you'll need a higher level of insight.

Look at different types of success

Entrepreneurs like myself often have many opportunities happening all at different stages, which means you may reach your goal with two medium-sized clients versus the big whale you've been trying to score. Does that affect the outcome? Run through a few ways success could happen for you. You may be surprised at how a slightly different outcome will affect your post-success strategy.

10
GOING PUBLIC
Recognition does not equal success

I'll never forget when my journalism law professor, the late Richard Schwarzlose, recommended I get E. B. White's *The New Journalism*. I was halfway through Northwestern's prestigious Magazine Publishing graduate program and realized that I didn't want to publish magazines. I wanted to write. "Go find *The New Journalism*" he said with a pat. "And you'll see what's possible." Published in 1973, *The New Journalism* had excerpts from edgy non-fiction writers who incorporated fiction techniques to unparalled effect. Tom Wolfe, Joan Didion, and Gay Talese were among them and are still considered literary giants today. I slept with the book under my pillow.

The most outrageous contributor was Hunter S. Thompson, the scoundrel who got in deep with The Hell's Angels, revealed southern racism at the Kentucky Derby, and truly exposed the dark side of Las Vegas. He consistently reported while being drunk and high and anti-social. He also was a master of words. To the untrained eye, it would be easy to assume that the former somehow enabled the latter. That would be a lie.

When Hunter S. Thompson died of an apparent suicide in 2005, one of his most shared quotes was from an old 1974 *Playboy Magazine* interview:

"One day you just don't appear at the El Adobe bar anymore: You shut the door, paint the windows black, rent an electric typewriter and become the monster you always were – the writer."

In other words, behind Thompson's drunken binges and crazy partying was sober work. It is always work. It will always be work. Work is behind everything.

Today, it isn't necessarily cocaine sniffs and tequila chasers. It is tweeting about the next novel you are going to do when you haven't written the last five books you've talked about. It is launching a kickstarter campaign for something you know you don't have the passion to follow through on. It is networking at conferences, at parties, and at coffeeshops about your brilliant idea that you could have – should have – started literally years ago. It is the flash before the fire, the dessert before the main course.

It is cheating.

We worry about selling out for security or big bucks, but the most dangerous selling out is you removing the work and soaking in the fun and the accolades that are supposed to be a reward for that very work. There is mounting scientific proof that saying you are going to do something and getting props for it taps the same part of your brain that recognizes reward for actually *doing* it. In other words, you could lose the motivation to achieve your goal simply because you've already gotten part of the reward: Recognition.

The results are sad. It is the drunk journalist who doesn't know what questions to ask, it is the potential writer posting endlessly about the new book he should be drafting, and it is the wannabe entrepreneur publicizing an app that they haven't even started developing. What they fail to understand is that the real spoils aren't recognition, awards, or money, but growth, insight, and impact – and that only comes with work.

There is no hack to that.

11
DIRTY WORK
Get your hands dirty as much as possible

My best entrepreneurial moments happened when I was tasked something I had no business doing. In creating my first app, So Quotable, I spent the first few years getting lots of support from a tech-savvy friend. One random day before it was going to launch, this person disappeared without a trace – and with the code. I was pissed. So, while taking care of my newborn baby, I learned to program for Apple devices, designed the user interface, and released the app within four months. It came out in time for my first TED Talk.

As my co-founders and I launched my second app, Cuddlr, circumstances shifted my role from a silent media and cultural strategist to the public face of the app. By the time we were acquired a year later, I was doing the majority of the interviews.

I'm proud of how I rose to those occasions, but I share this because I am 100 percent, absolutely positive that I wouldn't have done any of this unless it was necessary. Who in their right mind would get up before dawn to program with one hand while rocking their infant in the other? No one, that's who.

When I talked to my best friend, author A. Raymond Johnson, about the So Quotable experience, I compared it to being a lounge singer that suddenly became a singer-songwriter. I always had a vision, but now I could see the concept, map it out, and release it my damn self. I was a one-man band. I was free. My experience with Cuddlr essentially doubled down on that feeling, as I led our tiny company through intense media blitzes, demanding customers, and an eventual acquisition. They were journeys that few entrepreneurs are able to experience from inside the arena.

You may not be able to afford a capable programmer, a strong PR team, or a great logo artist. It may be late nights of you proverbially mopping the floor, taking out the trash, and doing the dishes by hand. But when you eventually are able to hire others to help, you'll have an unmistakably keen vision for how to run your business efficiently and wisely.

It is an insight the suckers who simply hired out the dirty work will never, ever have.

12

SKIP MONDAY

Strategize early to better execute later

It usually happens around Sunday afternoon: The vague, uncomfortable reminder that tomorrow is Monday. You get revved up to start the week at your A-game, but the pressure can often crush any real or perceived progress. It can be a rough cycle.

Instead, consider shifting your usual Monday work to Tuesday. Whether your business is based on the traditional work week or loosely framed around consultant hours, it is a simple strategy that can save you both time and anxiety.

No one is paying attention on Monday
When do brands announce things they don't want to get attention? Friday afternoon. And despite the norm, I'd argue that Monday morning would be a close second, as everyone is antsy to get out what they've been working on or

thinking about since late last week. The same can be said for important internal and external meetings, major sales launches and anything else that requires serious attention. It's like we all have a gag order for two and a half days and, suddenly, we have the opportunity to talk. Things quiet down by Tuesday morning - making the second day of the week perfect to make your announcement or to have a conversation.

No one is ready for Monday

Office Space clichés aside, we have to do a mental shift after two days off. Even if, like me, you work over the weekend, there's a difference between quietly getting things done and manning the workday phone, email and social media. Respect that you, and most every one else, are still in second gear. Treat Monday as you would Friday: Laying the groundwork for the upcoming days, but leaving the serious thought and actions to later.

No one is listening on Monday

When it comes to connecting with others, Monday is a pretty rough day. Monday is considered one of the weakest days to post on social media (Wednesday, arguably, is the best) as well as one of the worst days to cold call (Friday takes the award here). Save your heavy discussions and your "asks" for another day. Tuesday is an excellent candidate.

No one is satisfied with his or her progress on Monday

As a 5-day culture, we create this immense pressure to be as productive as possible every week. It may motivate you sometimes, but any less than stellar work or unfinished business comes back to bite us in the behind on Monday. It's like the Ghost of Friday's Past begins haunting on Sunday night - and by Monday morning, you are feeling the weight to make up even more for last week's lackluster productivity (even if it isn't actually lackluster). The expectation of bigger, better results can be an internal struggle or, worse, projected onto other people, including employees and colleagues, which means that even if you don't feel that way on Monday, there are others that are struggling. Why not sidestep the melodrama? Make a simple, limited list of what must get done on Monday, create a dialog with others enforcing the focused approach and save the heavy lifting for a less psychologically day: Tuesday.

13
TOO BUSY
Being too busy shows poor business vision

Based on our most common conversations, busyness today is an epidemic--even more so than it was for previous generations with less technology available. In fact, it can be a point of pride.

The truth is that we are not too busy; we just have too many choices to make clear priorities. One of the worst things you can say to someone in business is that you "are too busy."

Unfortunately, other people may be smart enough to understand your real message, even if you don't realize it yourself.

You don't care.

It's OK, as you can't care about everything--the very nature of something being a priority is that other things are less cared about. The first step, though, is to know yourself well enough to understand that you don't really care. The next step is to find a gentle way to say no.

You are inefficient.

Perhaps the most damning view is that you simply can't handle your business time efficiently. This perception goes double for fellow entrepreneurs: Many of us launched successful startups while juggling other personal and professional commitments. We're the last people you want to tell "I'm too busy." Instead, explain that you're working hard to give excellent attention to your current projects and, if possible, you will make room for other projects in the future.

You aren't serious about your business.
How many times do successful businesspeople turn down work? Quite often, actually, but it is because of their clarity of focus, not their busy schedule. It is a novice move to burn bridges or close doors prematurely, as your busy season today may turn into a slow churn tomorrow.

14
A Gentle "No"
Saying "no" is more important than saying "yes"

Rejection is a part of business, particularly entrepreneurship, but the biggest, most important rejections have to come from you. You can't accept every offer. You can't pursue every idea. You can't please every customer.

Unfortunately, between our "winner takes all" mentality and our fear of turning away work, we rarely develop the skills necessary to say No. In fact, saying No is easy. Stopping an action without destroying a potential future relationship is hard.

Here are three strong, kind and honest ways to say no--and actually learn about potential collaborators in the process:

"**When we work together, I want to make sure you have my full attention.**"

One of my biggest pet peeves is when a business partner commits to working together, but obviously has too much on his plate. The problem is that I do my best to make sure that I'm not overextended so he gets the attention and details deserved - and I assume others do the same.

"I need to respect those to whom I've already committed."

It reminds me of the adage "If someone gossips to you about other people, you can bet they are gossiping about you to other people." The same could be said for other business dealings: People who are unwilling to say No to you, even though they know they can't give you quality time, are the same people who will willingly sacrifice their commitment to you to work with someone else to whom they can't say No.

A potential collaborator may not like that you are prioritizing others' previous needs over their current needs, but they should respect it. If they don't respect your commitment to others, then that often reflects their own principles - and it may be a warning sign to keep in the back of your mind.

"We should make sure the timing is good."
Your business should naturally evolve, whether it means changing your product scope or identifying a new customer base. It means yesterday's great projects are today's misfires and last year's potential partnerships are now pretty lukewarm. There are amazing collaborators, clients and mentors I would love to work with right now, but as I focus in on my core business, I've had to gently let them know that our time to work together isn't here... yet. It leaves the door open for later opportunities and also confirms that you respect other people's time and are keen not to waste it.

"There's no problem with being where you are right now. We can be where we are and at the same time leave wide open the possibility of being able to expand far beyond where we are now in the course of our lifetime."

-Pema Chodron, Comfortable With Uncertainty

15

EMBRACE LIMITATION

Limited resources foster creativity and genius

I wrote about a dozen books over seven years, so it isn't unusual for others to talk to me about their ambitions to write. Overall I found that the biggest reason people haven't written a book yet is not a lack of literacy, nor the inability to understand publishing (indeed, you can Google self-publishing resources and have a book out by next week). The excuse was always something intangible, that things just hadn't come together yet.

"I haven't found the time.", "I need money to do it right.", "I am not living in the right place to really promote it."

Often, these are lies we tell ourselves. As we discussed in LIES WE TELL, "You will always need more resources than you have, more time than you got and more energy than you can muster. If Jobs, Musk and other visionaries waited until everything was perfect, then we wouldn't be talking about Jobs, Musk and their contemporaries right now."

Those books as well as major consulting gigs and even my last acquired startup were all done under some kind of resource poverty: Time, money or location. Call me crazy, but those actually made the opportunities not only better, but increased the chances of those opportunities actually showing up.

Personal scarcity

Isn't it amazing how we manage to get our projects done just in the nick of time, no matter how long the deadline? We always pace ourselves, expanding and contracting our productivity, based on the time available. Our biggest constraints are often personal: Relationship needs like our families, physical needs like our rest, or emotional needs like our hobbies. After having my first kid, my workweek was slashed from 60 hours to about 15 hours - and I launched two startups, did two TED talks and blossomed my career while being his primary caretaker. It's not about time, but efficiency.

Financial scarcity
We may dream about being billionaires, but complete financial freedom can actually be a detriment to productivity. Artists and entrepreneurs often thrive when they have fewer resources simply because they must be more creative and innovative. Waiting until your money is better is often a mistake.

Location scarcity
It's not about Silicon Valley. I have meet fascinating entrepreneurs in nontraditional areas like Cincinnati, Detroit, and Miami aiming to put their city on the map or bring it back to past glory. I also know entrepreneurs who are sitting on their laurels until they can

move to a major city, which is akin to an author waiting until they meet an agent to type any words. The question is, where can you make the most impact?

16

MARTYRDOM

Sacrificing your well being won't help your business

Passion usually gets us into our entrepreneurial profession, as there would be little other reason for us to take such giant risks. It's a double-edged sword, though, as passion can make us push ourselves too hard. It also can have us make short-term decisions that don't make any sense for our well-being or, ironically, for our actual long-term business.

We should expect to make adjustments within specific periods - people call it "crunch time". For instance, I spent more than a year getting up in the wee hours of the night to launch my startups and my speaking career, but I put a set time limit on that insane schedule, which helped me stay balanced throughout. Unfortunately, it is way too easy to begin sacrificing important things and making crisis mode your default. Here are the big three parts of your life that are not worth putting at the sacrificial altar.

Sleep

I'm guilty as charged on this one, which is why I can speak from experience. Media mogul Arianna Huffington has written a best-selling book on the importance of sleep. Jeff Bezos, who is easily controlling half of your online commerce, gets eight hours a night. Science has proven that it is more productive to get more sleep and work less than it is to do the opposite (and why a nap should be on your daily agenda).

Food

A "nutritious" shake may save 15 minutes time, but it doesn't give your mind and body the break it needs to process problems nor to rest between intense work blocks. Not eating at all is truly a recipe for disaster, and the older we get, the less our bodies will tolerate the stress.

Relationships
What's funny is that we never really sacrifice our relationships, but just burn out our social currency. You become the friend that only calls when she needs something (and, as an entrepreneur, you will definitely eventually need something). Not cultivating and managing your relationships ends up hurting your business growth - doing the opposite of what you may claim you're not cultivating and managing your relationships for.

17
SCARY VACATIONS
Never stopping isn't a sign of strength, but of fear

Legendary entrepreneur Elon Musk recently shared a private issue with the press: He is afraid of taking a break. He was quoted as saying:

The first time I took a week off, the Orbital Sciences rocket exploded and Richard Branson's rocket exploded. In that same week, the second time I took a week off, my rocket exploded. The lesson here is don't take a week off.

It may be a brilliantly logical man showing his superstitious side, but his phobia of vacation echoes what many of us believe: You can't afford to stop. Evidence now shows that you can't afford not to stop, but there are many reasons why you believe you can't have or don't deserve a break.

You don't have the structure in place

Have you enabled your business enough so you can actually be unavailable for a few days? Very few of us have. It goes beyond vacation, though: Personally, unexpected health issues and family emergencies have put my own work at a standstill. Enabling co-workers, subordinates, or even our brain trusts is key to feeling better about taking a break. It also requires putting your ego aside and realizing that denying yourself time to recharge doesn't equate "crushing it" as an entrepreneur.

You fear competitors will quickly leave you in the dust

Often in our minds, competitors are No-Doz snorting freaks of nature that never rest. They are just waiting for us to pause so they can take the lead. Even the noblest professions have a ruthless edge, but stopping actually can give our minds the chance to create the strategy we need to win.

The greatest entrepreneur of our generation, Steve Jobs, took infamously long walk breaks. Stopping also prevents us from tinkering too much on our products. Finally, we are less likely to go to extreme thinking and ruin what we've spent so much time building.

You are afraid of facing what you've left behind

Startups can easily demand all of our time, to the point that many of us have given up on having any type of healthy social or family life. But what happens when your business closes or you have a successful exit and you have nothing else to focus on but your life outside of work? It's a scary thought, especially if there is a trail of broken promises and strained relationships laying in your ambitious wake. Unfortunately, avoiding personal conflict just prolongs, if not exacerbates the issues that aren't being addressed. Facing those demons is akin to the popular proverb about planting trees: "The best time to do it would be 20 years ago. The second best time to do it would be today."

When is the last time you actually stopped?

18

THE SMARTEST PERSON
Your network really is your net worth

We create startups with the idealistic
intention of building a community
around it, yet often don't take the time
to create a community within our own
personal entrepreneurship. This
dawned on me when I was in Silicon
Valley and, organically, my friends and
I had created our own brain trust.

A hodge podge of techies, entrepreneurs
and artists, we'd gather together every
week to drink, connect, and recap. It
became a magnet, as regulars would
inevitably have a friend in town or
another colleague interested in coming
through and they, too, would stop by
whenever possible. The diversity in
people pushed our conversations
beyond any discussions we could have
had in a less public forum.

I left the Bay Area a while ago, but I'm

still connected to the valuable people I met. Now we've spun off into interesting ventures, like tackling Silicon Valley diversity and leading the discussion on tech's human impact. More than that, they became the trusted colleagues and mentors for my startup adventures.

In short, they are my brain trust: A diverse, collective sounding board for my next entrepreneurial moves. And every entrepreneur should have one.

Do you have people to listen to your ideas and help you take things to the next level? Here's how you can cultivate them.

Rise to the occasion

As the saying goes, if you're the smartest person in the room, then you need to go find a better room. Your collective should push you to be more strategic, more ambitious and more successful, rather than stroke your ego based on past actions.

Being around smart, accomplished people will push you to higher heights. Attending my first TED Conference was both thrilling and intimidating, but the experience turned me into a regular attendee and, a few years later, a TED speaker myself. Connecting with the American Society of Journalists and Authors made me realize how much further I could go with my writing, inspiring me to become an active member and eventually join its Board of Directors. You should connect with people who help you recognize and encourage you to be your highest self.

Make the time

Our lives can be a blur of late nights/early mornings, airport hopping and crunch times. Cultivating a reliable set of colleagues and mentors should be built into your schedule, just as you would make time for strategic planning or for budget allocation.

Consider the return on investment. I recently offered to take a wise colleague out for an expensive meal. What I got was advice that helped me wrap up my startup gracefully. The priceless insight not only required me setting aside time for the dinner, but also energy building and cultivating the relationship to the point where I could have a long dinner with them. Relationships take time.

Talk to folks in other disciplines

Artists can often be bad businesspeople not because they are awful at math, but because they don't mingle with MBAs and accountants who could give them advice. It is easy to stay in the comfort zone and, as we get older, it gets harder to leave it.

Connecting with different professionals becomes even more important after we get established. Early in our career, we are eager for leads, feedback and direction. As our work stabilizes, though, we think we already have the contacts we need and assume the work will continue to flow. It's not until we need the insight of an advertising specialist, or a media journalist, or another highly-focused professional outside of our field that we realize how narrow our circle has become. You don't want to be facing a difficult business decision and have no one to give you an informed opinion on it.

How are you building a reliable entrepreneurial community for yourself?

19
BE BORED
Not doing encourages daring ideas

We talk today about powering through pain, fatigue, and exhaustion to reach our entrepreneurial goals, but sometimes stopping is exactly what we need to do to understand what we should be doing next. And stopping, sometimes, requires being bored.

Best-selling The Personal MBA author Josh Kaufman explained it well on entrepreneur Tara Gentile's *Profit Power Pursuit* podcast:

I'm actually thinking about taking the Internet out of my office entirely. The more you can make it harder for yourself to focus on anything else, that's valuable. I think there's a lot to be said for "strategic boredom". Just removing all the other things that could be potential distractions... just get rid of them temporarily. And if you can make what you want to do the most interesting thing that you have in your environment, then a lot more gets done that way.

Kaufman calls it "strategic boredom". Whatever you are doing, whether it is a strategy session, a pitch deck or a new manuscript, has to be the most interesting thing happening in your world at that moment. Your social media timeline, mindless busy work and other potential distractions have no place here. Personally, I've found my own work elevated when I minimize the amount of focal points I have - which sometimes means physically unplugging the Internet.

When is the last time you allowed yourself to be bored? If you can't imagine it, then you likely fear it. Here are three reasons why it scares us.

We waste time being afraid of wasting time

Boredom is considered a bad thing today, as we associate it with unproductivity. We always want to feel like we are busy by being on social media, going on business trips, or doing all-nighters for the business. However, our most insightful strategies and ideas happen when we are walking somewhere, taking a moment to think or actually resting for a moment.

In fact, a recent study cited by the Harvard Business Review found that we are more productive when we take time to look at nature. Having been raised in the city, I associated nature with boredom well into adulthood, as perhaps you did, too. As the study shows, though, nature is really a catalyst for us to pause and access the moment. It gives our brains a chance to process and strategize--and avoid potentially time-wasting moves in the future.

We worry that inaction will make things fall apart

The entrepreneurial world seems to operate on two gears: Stop or Run. You are either running towards profitability or paddling to stay afloat. It is extreme thinking, and it is what keeps us willingly sacrificing our health and our relationships to reach another business milestone.

Crunch time is real, but insane hours, emotional stress, and ridiculous malnutrition are meant for significant stretches, not as the default. Is every moment crucial? Probably not, or your definition of crucial isn't really valid. The truth is that our ego wants to believe that we are sacrificing everything at this moment because it is what is required of us to succeed. Working without pause also helps us avoid boredom, and that very silence that would make us face the truth about the decisions we've made and the ones we keep on making.

We fear we aren't good enough, so we tinker when we shouldn't

The fear of boredom also means that we will mess with things when we really should let them flow naturally. Picture the nervous artist fussing over a painting that is already done or a businessperson aggressively addressing a harmless contractual point at the last minute. We have the ability to destroy all our hard work simply because we can't just sit still and shut up.

Mounting scientific evidence says that creatives--the risk takers and the entrepreneurs--are more likely to overthink their ideas and strategies to the point of neurosis. The deck is already stacked against us. Don't be your own worst enemy.

20
AFTER THE WIN
We are most vulnerable after a success

If we love anything, then it is talking about the struggle to succeed. It is about being focused, about showing up every day and about potentially betting the farm to win.

But what happens after we win? Well, a lot happens.

Entrepreneur Toni Ko felt lost after she sold her cosmetics company to L'oreal for a reported $500 million. Co-founder Marc Lore felt disappointment when his company was acquired by Amazon for $550 million. I went through my own challenges after my popular app, Cuddlr, was acquired.

The toughest part, though, is allowing ourselves to struggle again in our next pursuit. That's why we are more likely to fail after we win big. And it often isn't the positive, swing for the fences failure, but the soul crushing kind. *The Ego is the Enemy* author Ryan Holiday shared exactly why with entrepreneur Tim Ferriss:

Ego is dangerous when you're aspiring to something, no question, but when you are successful and you've built this thing and then you're trying to do your next thing, when you're convinced that everything you touch turns to gold, that's where ego is the most destructive.

It breaks down into a couple reasons. First, your ego, like all of our egos, is insatiable and is hungry for more praise. It is the equivalent of the lab rat being given a sugar cube: It is fine beforehand but, once the sweet treat is introduced, it will get agitated and angry if it doesn't get it again.

We have to train ourselves not to take our success as the default. Instead, the practice of our work should be the default.

Second, you have taken your mastery for granted. Do you remember the first time you started your profession? I started crafting stories when I was a toddler, so I seriously cannot remember when I began narrating to an audience. The longer you've been doing something, the less you remember the pain, struggle and hard work it initially required. It is why you should diversify your social circles and create side hustles to make sure you are not mentally complacent.

The best cure? Always be a beginner at something.

21
WE NEED YOU
No one can duplicate your unique genius

I spent a remarkable amount of time studying astrology, and I blame Kelby, my first "girlfriend". Cresting and ending as a high school summer over-the-phone-only romance, our relationship was mostly talking about how different we were and how, astrologically, we weren't supposed to work. Around that time, I saw Linda Goodman's *Star Signs* on my grandmother's shelf. I read it several times that summer, from top to bottom, and began reading other books about astrology, which led me to Carl Jung, the Myers-Briggs Test, and more sociology.

Many years later, I'm a broke post-grad student living as a freelance writer in Chicago. I get some stuff published, but I can barely make my apartment rent which was decided based on a job opportunity that vanished. As I reached my wits' end, a friend of a friend connected me with a major online portal. It was looking for editorial content and wondered what I could write about. I highlighted technology, video games, sexuality and – screw it – astrology. It immediately hired me as an astrologist, pulling in a salary that I would even consider decent today. And I had some of the most fun ever as a freelancer. I had no idea.

Stuart Butterfield and his partners just made a mint selling the photo website they founded, Flickr, and decided to reinvest some of it into creating a video game company. They wanted to specifically focus on the online experience. Unfortunately, they invested millions into the PC realm right when mobile was rising. Realizing their folly, the founders had a hard conversation with investors and decided to shut down the company. The investors were in deep, too, at least $17 million. The founders had a meeting laying off virtually the entire team, during which Butterfield burst into tears. The founders went back to the drawing board.

While they were working on the game, though, they created an elaborate internal chat system that allowed them to quickly communicate and share files with each other. With nothing to lose, they began sharing the chat system with friends at Microsoft and other companies. The team was surprised at the response and realized that their little side project, not their robust video game, was the real hit. They named it Slack. By Summer 2016, Slack was the defacto corporate chat choice and was worth $4 billion. It was only four years old. Butterfield had no idea.

Let's talk about you. The crazy idea in your head may be the very next thing the world needs. There is no use in waiting for a sign (unless you absolutely need to, which, in that case, consider this your sign.) You can't rely on timing, as it may take you weeks, months, or even years to do your thing, and you have no idea what the world will look like at that moment. You can't rely on others, as no one else shares the exact vision you have, so no one else can tell you whether to go forward or not. And you can't rely on the past, as doing more of what was done yesterday is a waste of all of our time, particularly yours.

What you can do is listen to that nagging voice that is telling you that you have a higher purpose. What you can do is begin moving towards that higher purpose. What you can do is start walking. Today.

Steven Presssfield sums it up well in his classic book *The War of Art*:

"Creative work is not a selfish act or a bit for attention on the part of the actor. It's a gift to the world and every being in it. Don't

cheat us of your contribution."

What are you being called to contribute right now?

TAKING IT TO THE NEXT LEVEL

FREE VIDEOS & ARTICLES: WWW.BITESIZED.BIZ
TWITTER/INSTAGRAM: *@BROWNDAMON*
CONSULTING & SPEAKING REQUESTS:
DAMON@DAMONBROWN.NET

Bring Damon to your startup, incubator or organization for one of these popular keynote talks:

WHY YOU CAN (AND SHOULD) START YOUR SIDE HUSTLE IMMEDIATELY-KEYNOTE

Believe it or not, we already have most of the skills we need to create our passion- driven business. So why aren't most people pursuing their potentially profitable ideas? They are intimidated by the small gap in their skill set. In this immediately actionable talk, Damon shares how to easily traverse that gap and explains the three crucial strengths every successful entrepreneur possesses. It is an inspiring talk for both potential entrepreneurs and ambitious upstarts.

115

5 WAYS TO DO MORE IN LESS TIME - KEYNOTE

We all want more time for our most passionate ideas, but we often don't even get started because we want to wait until we have more space in our schedule. Meanwhile, our best ideas could be dying on the vine. In a smart, practical talk, Damon gives five brilliant strategies that will maximize your time and boost your productivity. The actionable ideas are great for professionals, leaders, and students.

I look forward to connecting with you!

Significant Quotes & References

- Table of Contents:
  - Opening quote: Steven Pressfield, "The Unlived Life", from *The War of Art* (Black Irish Entertainment, 2012)
- Chapter 1
  - Opening quote: Steven Pressfield, "Resistance is Infallible", from *The War of Art* (Black Irish Entertainment, 2012)
  - Jessica Abel quote: Jessica Abel, "Don't Find Your Passion". Originally published May 26, 2016
  - Adapted from the *Inc.* column "Forget Inspiration. This Beats Passion Every Single Time". Originally published June 16, 2016

- Chapter 2: Lies We Tell
  - Adapted from the *Inc.* columns "Lies Entrepreneurs Tell Themselves" and "Big Lies Entrepreneurs Tell Themselves". Originally published August 15, 2015 and October 19, 2015
- Chapter 3: Effective Procrastination
  - Jessica Hirsche quote: Quoted by Animaux Circus, 2016
  - Adapted from the *Inc.* column "How Procrastination Can Supercharge Your Business". Originally published December 21, 2015
- Chapter 4: Idea Debt
  - Kazu Kibuishi quote: Jessica Abel, "Imagine your future projects holding you back".

Originally published
January 27, 2016
- o Adapted from the *Inc.*
  column "Why Your
  Brilliant Ideas Are
  Holding You Back".
  Originally published
  February 28, 2016
- Chapter 5: Busyness
  - o Adapted from the *Inc.*
    column "3 Awful Reasons
    Why You Are Obsessed
    with Being Busy".
    Originally published April
    13, 2016
- Chapter 6: A Good Burnout
  - o Adapted from the *Inc.*
    column "How You Can
    Turn Burnout To Your
    Advantage". Originally
    published October 23, 2015

- Chapter 7: Clutter
  - o Damon Brown quote: Damon Brown, "Death by Curation: The problem with recording everything", adapted from *Our Virtual Shadow* (TED Books 2013). Originally published September 2, 2013.
  - o Adapted from the *Inc.* column "The 2 Types of Clutter Stalling Your Business". Originally published July 24, 2015
- Chapter 8: Growth Spurt
  - o Opening quote: Brene Brown, "Chapter One: The Physics of Vulnerability", from *Rising Strong* (Spiegel & Grau, 2015)
  - o Adapted from the *Inc.* column "How to Turn a Growth Spurt Into a Triumph". Originally published March 7, 2016

- Chapter 9: Favors the Prepared
  - Adapted from the *Inc.* column "Why Not Preparing for Success is the Ultimate Failure". Originally published February 26, 2016
- Chapter 10: Going Public
  - Hunter S. Thompson quote: Craig Vetter, *Playboy Magazine*, "Playboy Interview: Hunter Thompson". Originally published November 1974
- Chapter 12: Skip Monday
  - Adapted from the *Inc.* column "Tuesday Should Be Your New Monday". Originally published November 16, 2015

- Chapter 13: Too Busy
    - Adapted from the *Inc.* column "The Message You're Really Sending With 'I'm Too Busy'". Originally published June 14, 2016
- Chapter 14: A gentle "No"
    - Adapted from the *Inc.* column "3 Smart, Strategic Ways to Say No and Save Your Business Relationships". Originally published March 1, 2016
- Chapter 15: Embrace Limitation
    - Opening quote: Pema Chodron, "Be Where You Are", *from Comfortable With Uncertainty* (Shambhula, 2003)
    - Adapted from the *Inc.* column "Why Difficult Limitations Make You a Better Entrepreneur". Originally published May 12, 2016

- Chapter 16: Martyrdom
  - Adapted from the *Inc.* column "Sacrificing Yourself for Your Business is Silly and Useless". Originally published June 16, 2016
- Chapter 17: Scary Vacations
  - Adapted from the *Inc.* column "Why Entrepreneurs Like Elon Musk Fear Vacations". Originally published October 7, 2015
- Chapter 18: The Smartest Person
  - Adapted from the *Inc.* column "Why You Need a Brain Trust". Originally published September 25, 2015

- Chapter 19: Be Bored
  - Josh Kaufman quote: *Profit Power Pursuit, a Creative Live Podcast, with Tara Gentile*, "Episode 033: Josh Kaufman". Originally aired May 24, 2016
  - Adapted from the *Inc.* column "Why Strategic Boredom Will Boost Your Productivity". Originally published May 31, 2016
- Chapter 20: After the Win
  - Ryan Holiday quote: *The Tim Ferriss Show*, "Useful Lessons from Workaholics Anonymous, Corporate Implosions, and More", Originally aired June 25, 2016
  - Adapted from the *Inc.* column "Why Most People Fail Immediately After a Big Success". Originally published July 7, 2016

- Chapter 21
  - Steven Pressfield quote: Steven Pressfield, "The Artist's Life", from *The War of Art* (Black Irish Entertainment, 2012)
  - Adapted from the *Inc.* column "Destroy Average Ideas to Make Brilliant Manure". Originally published March 9, 2016

ACKNOWLEDGMENTS

This book wouldn't exist without some awesome (mis)adventures in entrepreneurship. A hat tip to geniuses in my midst, including Chia Hwu, Monique Woodard, David Goldenberg, Christina Brodbeck, Atul Techchandani, and Mark McGuire, as well as past and present partners, including my Cuddlr co-founder Charlie Williams. A special blessing to my partnerships that ended poorly; thank you for the lessons.

Articulating the transition from journalist to entrepreneur would have been much more difficult without great sounding boards like E. B. Boyd, Peter Economy, Minda Zetlin, Andrea King Collier, Randy Dotinga, Mary Beth Temple, Evelyn Kane, A. Raymond Johnson, and Stephan Garnett.

A big shout to my long-time accountability partner (e.g. goal buddy) Jeanette Hurt for editing and artist Bec

Loss for the cover – thanks for your patience! Also my insightful colleagues in the publishing industry, particularly Marilyn Allen and Chris Barsanti.

Love to Steven Pressfield, Brene Brown, and Pema Chodron. I hope to make even a shred of the significant impact you have made on millions of artists, dreamers, and creators.

Special thanks to *Inc. Magazine*'s Laura Lorber, Douglas Cantor, and Kevin Ryan for supporting the growth of our Sane Success column, which inspired this book. IDG's Jim Malone and Jennifer Dionne, *Four Seasons Magazine*'s Alicia Miller and Waynette Goodson, and ET's Shana Krochmal were priceless allies, too.

And finally, thanks to my entrepreneurial parents, Bernadette Johnson and David Brown, and my wife, Dr. Parul Patel, as well as our boys Alec and Abhi. I love you.

ABOUT THE AUTHOR

Damon Brown is a long-time journalist and author of several books, most notably *Our Virtual Shadow: Why We Are Obsessed with Documenting Our Lives Online* (TED Books 2013) and *Porn & Pong: How Grand Theft Auto, Tomb Raider and Other Sexy Games Changed Our Culture* (Feral House 2008), as well as the coffeetable book *Playboy's Greatest Covers* (Sterling Publishing 2012). *The Bite-Sized Entrepreneur* is his 17th book.

Damon co-founded the social meetup app Cuddlr while being the primary caretaker to his infant. It went number one on the Apple App store twice, changing the cultural conversation around platonic intimacy. The app was acquired less than a year after it launched, and the whirlwind experience inspired Damon's popular *Inc.com* column Sane Success as well as *The Bite-Sized Entrepreneur*.

You can catch Damon in *Playboy*, *Fast Company*, and *Entrepreneur*, as well as at any locale that serves really spicy food. He lives in Southern California with his wife, two young sons, and countless bottles of hot sauce.

Connect with him at www.damonbrown.net or on Twitter at @browndamon.

Manufactured by Amazon.com
Columbia, SC
30 March 2017